Feelings

I'm Happy
and other fun feelings

Clare Hibbert
Illustrated by Simona Dimitri

Evans

Published by Evans Brothers Limited
2A Portman Mansions, Chiltern Street, London W1U 6NR

© Evans Brothers Limited 2010
Concept devised for Evans Brothers by Clare Hibbert

Editor: Clare Hibbert
Designer: Sandra Perry
Picture researcher: Sophie Schrey
Illustrator: Simona Dimitri (Milan Illustration Agency)
Sign language artist: Rob Perry

British Library Cataloguing in Publication Data
Hibbert, Clare, 1970-
Happy. – (Feelings)
1. Happiness–Juvenile literature.
I. Title II. Series
152.4'2-dc22

ISBN-13: 9780237541989

Printed & bound in China by New Era Printing Co. Ltd.

**The signing instructions in this book follow British Sign Language.
The visual instructions show a mirror image to make it easier for
you to practise your own signing in front of a mirror.**

CONTENTS

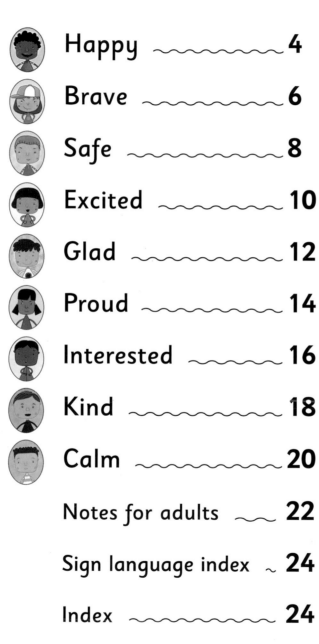

Happy

I played at the park with my friends. I felt **happy**.

yippee!

happy

brave

safe

excited

4

wheeeee

Whooosh!

glad

proud

interested

kind

calm

5

Brave

In my game I fought a dragon. I felt very **brave**.

Swish

Roooooar!

calm

Safe

choo choo!

happy   brave   safe   excited

My friend doesn't like big groups. But when he's with me, he feels **safe**.

clatter

glad

proud

interested

kind

calm

9

Excited

happy birthday to you!

My friend invited me to her party. I was very **excited**.

10

happy

brave

safe

excited

glad proud interested kind calm

11

Glad

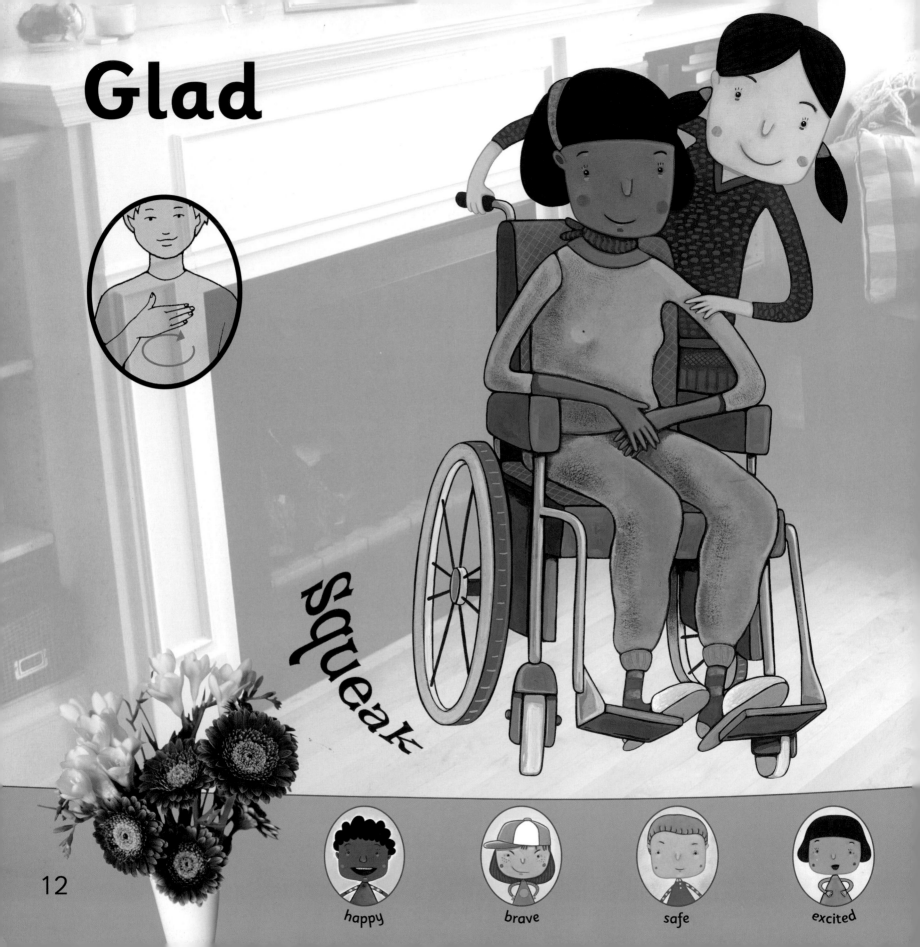

squeak

happy   brave   safe   excited

WELCOME HOME

My neighbour came out of hospital. I felt **glad**.

trundle

glad

proud

interested

kind

calm

13

Proud

I made Grandad **proud**. He was a good swimmer too.

14

happy

brave

safe

excited

splish splash!

glad   proud   interested   kind   calm

15

Interested

eeek! WOW!

happy

brave

safe

excited

I visited the museum with my class. I felt **interested**.

glad

proud

interested

kind

calm

Kind

echo, echo

I helped the new girl find her way. I felt **kind**.

tick tock

18

happy

brave

safe

excited

19

Calm

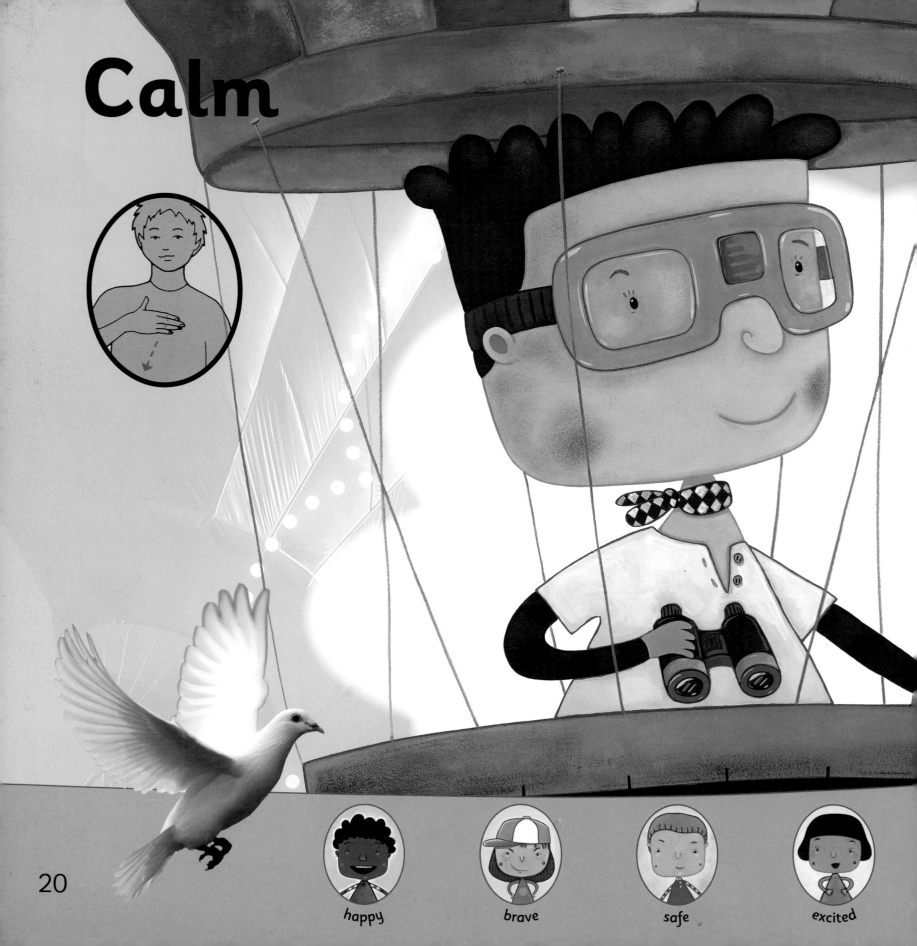

happy   brave   safe   excited

I was worried, so I thought of something **calm**.

whoosh

glad

proud

interested

kind

calm

Notes for adults

The **Feelings...** series has been designed to support and extend the learning of young children. The books link in to the Early Years curriculum and beyond. Find out more about Early Years and reading with children from the National Literacy Trust (www.literacytrust.org.uk).

The **Feelings...** series helps to develop children's knowledge, understanding and skills in key social and emotional aspects of learning (SEAL), in particular empathy, self-awareness and social skills. It aims to help children understand, articulate and manage their feelings. Visit http://nationalstrategies.standards.dcsf.gov.uk/node/87009 to find out more about SEAL.

Titles in the series:
I'm Happy and other fun feelings looks at positive emotions
I'm Sad and other tricky feelings looks at uncomfortable emotions
I'm Tired and other body feelings looks at physical feelings
I'm Busy a feelings story explores other familiar feelings

The **Feelings...** books offer the following special features:

1) **matching game**
   a border of expressive faces gives readers the chance to hunt out the face that matches the emotion covered on the spread;
2) **signing instructions**
   each spread includes clear visual instructions for signing the emotion (these follow British Sign Language standard – visit britishsignlanguage.com for more information about this organisation);
3) **fantasy scenes**
   since children often explore emotion through stories, dreams and their imaginations, two emotions (in this book, 'brave' and 'calm') are presented in a fantasy setting, giving the opportunity to examine intense feelings in the safety of an unreal context.

Making the most of reading time
When reading with younger children, take time to explore the pictures together. Ask children to find, identify, count or describe different objects. Point out colours and textures. Pause in your reading so that children can ask questions, repeat your words or even predict the next word. This sort of participation develops early reading skills.

Follow the words with your finger as you read. The main text is in Infant Sassoon, a clear, friendly font designed for children learning to read and write. The thought and speech bubbles and sound effects add fun and give the opportunity to distinguish between levels of communication.

Extend children's learning by using this book as a springboard for discussion and follow-on activities. Here are a few ideas:

Pages 4–5: I feel happy

Ask children to keep a happiness diary for a week. Divide a sheet of paper into seven areas, and write the names of the days. Each day, the children can record things that made them happy by drawing or sticking on something (for example an ice cream wrapper or a photo).

Pages 6–7: I feel brave

Use a selection of art materials to make a gigantic dragon mural – egg boxes make excellent 3D scales. Hunt out a retelling of 'George and the Dragon'. How many other dragon stories do the children know? Do they believe dragons are real or not? What other pretend monsters can they think of?

Pages 8–9: I feel safe

Discuss why someone might feel scared in the school or nursery setting. Think together of ways to make it safe and accessible to all. Could a mentoring system work?

Encourage the children to make clothes-pegs 'emotion dolls' that they can use to express difficult feelings and explore tricky situations, for example at circle time.

Pages 10–11: I feel excited

Stick 12 big circles on the wall. Label each with the name of a month. Ask each child to put a named drawing or photo of him- or herself in the correct birthday month (to adapt for home, show birthdays of family and friends). What other events in the year are exciting? Add illustrated markers for festivals such as Chinese New Year, Holi, Easter, Id-ul-Fitr, Divali, Hallowe'en, Guru Nanak, Christmas and Hanukkah.

Pages 12–13: I feel glad

Make up a simple 'welcome home' song – or teach the words to 'For s/he's a jolly good fellow'. Encourage the children to accompany the singing with a selection of percussion, and discuss how the joyful music expresses the feeling of gladness.

Pages 14–15: I feel proud

Cut out tinfoil circles and ask children to draw on simple icons to represent activities that they do well (such as a football, bicycle, paintbrush or pair of swimming goggles). Attach the 'medals of achievement' to coloured ribbons so they can be worn around the children's necks.

Pages 16–17: I feel interested

Can children think of the word that means the opposite of 'interested'? Children can create a pairs game by illustrating cards with opposite emotions or states, for example happy/sad, quiet/noisy, sleepy/wide awake, interested/bored.

Pages 18–19: I feel kind

Encourage children to draw a plan of their school or nursery to help newcomers find their way. Mark the entrance, and use pictures cut out from magazines to illustrate key places (for example the toilets, lunchroom, reading area and playground).

Pages 20–21: I feel calm

Ask each child to imagine a calm, happy scene that they can think about whenever they feel worried or frightened, for example after a bad dream. Then provide paints and collage materials so children can recreate their imaginings for a display.

Sign language

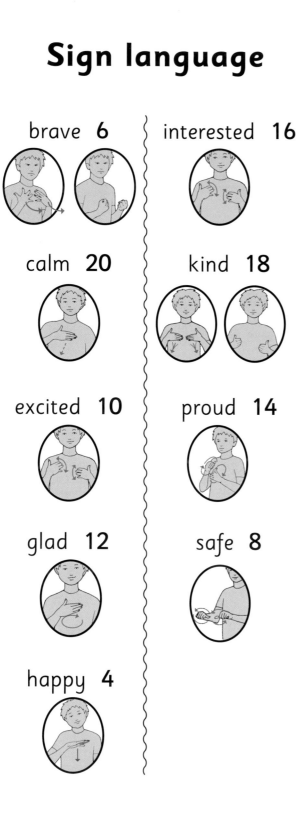

brave 6

interested 16

calm 20

kind 18

excited 10

proud 14

glad 12

safe 8

happy 4

Index

Credits

The publisher would like to thank the following for permission to reproduce their images:
iStockphoto: cover and 4–5 (Peter Garbet), 4 (Cebas), 6–7 (Dave Block), 6 (Stiggdriver), 8 (mammamaart), 10–11 (ptaxa), 10 (hidesy), 12–13 (Ramsey Blacklock), 12 (tirc83), 14–15 (Lugo Graphics), 14 (klikk), 16–17 (Jello5700), 18–19 (Eric Ferguson), 18 (VisualField), 21 (jacomstephens); **Shutterstock Images:** 7 (Sandra van der Steen), 8–9 (Hannamariah), 16 (zaharch), 20–21 (Centrill Media), 20 (Christopher Ewing).